Teachings on Je Tsongkhapa's

Three Principal Aspects of the Path

By

His Holiness the XIV Dalai Lama

Translated by

Ven. Lhakdor & Edited by Jeremy Russell

His Holiness gave this teaching at the request of a group of students from France in the main temple at Thekchen Choling in the Autumn of 1989

LIBRARY OF TIBETAN WORKS AND ARCHIVES

ISBN: 81-86470-42-5

Published by Library of Tibetan Works and Archives, Dharamsala
and printed at Indraprastha Press (CBT), 4 Bahadur Shah Zafar Marg,
New Delhi-110002

Contents

Contents

Preface

I am happy that the Library of Tibetan Works and Archives (LTWA) is publishing His Holiness the Dalai Lama's commentary on *The Three Principal Aspects of the Path*, which I had the fortune to simultaneously translate during the teaching itself, and later prepare this written translation with the help of my long-term friend Jeremy Russell. This is a text taught by Tsongkhapa to Tsakho Onpo Ngawang Dakpa in a place called Gyamo Rong in eastern Tibet.

The Three Principal Aspects of the Path are the axis or lifeline of all the sutric and tantric practices that you undertake. In other words, it is important that your practice be influenced by these three. For when your practice is influenced by renunciation, it becomes a cause for achieving liberation (Nirvana), when it is influenced by Bodhichitta it becomes a cause for achieving omniscience (Buddhahood), and when it is influenced by correct view it becomes an antidote to the cycle of existence (Samsara). In the absence of these main aspects of the path, even if one is well versed in the five subjects of learning, even if one is able to remain in a meditative state for many eons, even if one possesses the five clairvoyances, and even if one has achieved the eight great accomplishments, one will not be able to go beyond this cycle of existence.

The Three Principal Aspects of the Path are the essence of all the scriptures of the Buddha. The meaning of the Buddha's teachings and commentaries on them are included in the stages of the path of the three individuals and these in turn are included in the Three Principal Aspects of the Path. This is so because the purpose of all the scriptures containing the Buddha's teachings and their commentaries is really to help followers achieve Buddhahood. To attain that state of omniscience, one should practise the two-fold practice of skillful means and wisdom,

vi

within which the main practice is Bodhichitta and correct view (wisdom understanding emptiness). In order to cultivate these two, one should have first of all cultivated a deep sense of disgust towards the superficial marvels of the cycle of existence, and should have developed genuine renunciation—the wish to come out of samsara. In the absence of this, it is impossible to develop the great compassion which aspires to liberate other sentient beings from the cycle of existence. Hence renunciation is a must.

Bodhichitta is the main practice of accumulation of merit for achieving the body of the Buddha (Rupa Kaya), and correct view is the main practice for achieving the truth body (Dharmakaya). Moreover in the beginning, in order to convince one's mind to embrace dharma, one needs renunciation. To ensure that the dharma practice becomes a Mahayana path of practice, one needs Bodhichitta, and to eliminate completely the two obscurations, correct view is a must. Thus these three are known as the Three Principal Aspects of the Path. This way of practising all the essential points of the path by including them in these three principal aspects is a very special instruction that Manjushri gave directly to Tsongkhapa.

renunciat Bodh ichitta, Correct View

Lhakdor
DIRECTOR

Introduction

Today I am going to explain the *Three Principal Aspects of the Path*. As usual, before beginning a teaching, we will do the three practices for cleaning our mental continuums and then we will recite the Heart Sutra. Now make the mandala offering.

Whatever teachings are being given both the listener and the teacher should have a pure motivation. Especially when you listen to a Mahayana teaching, you should firstly take refuge in the Buddha, Dharma and Sangha to protect yourself from following the wrong path, and secondly you should generate an altruistic mind of enlightenment to differentiate yourself from followers of lower paths. Therefore we should visualise two points: firstly, taking refuge in the Buddha, Dharma and Sangha for the benefit of all sentient beings, then generating the altruistic aspiration to enlightenment for the sake of all sentient beings. So with this motivation, we should recite the verse for taking refuge in the Buddha, Dharma and Sangha three times, clearly visualising that we are doing so for the benefit of all sentient beings.

After the incomparable Buddha had attained enlightenment at the Bodh Gaya, he taught the Four Noble Truths: true sufferings, the true causes of suffering, true cessations and true paths. This became the basis or foundation for all the later teachings he gave. Although the Buddha taught the Four Noble Truths during his first turning of the wheel of the doctrine, the meaning of true cessation was most explicitly taught during the second turning of the wheel of doctrine. At that time, he taught the meaning of emptiness directly, and implicitly taught the stages of the path. In other words, while teaching emptiness directly, he taught the meaning of the two truths, conventional and ultimate truth, and the complete meaning of nirvana and cessation.

During the third turning of the wheel of doctrine, the Buddha taught the meaning of Buddha nature in the *Tathagata Essence Sutra*, that forms the basis for Maitreya's *Sublime Science (Uttaratantra)*. He explained that sentient beings have a Buddha nature or an ability to become enlightened mainly in terms of the nature of the mind, which is empty of inherent existence and thus suitable to be transformed into enlightenment. It is very clearly explained in the *Sublime Science* that the mind is by nature very pure and free of defilement which makes it suitable for attaining enlightenment. This is because anything which lacks inherent existence is changeable, and subject to causes and conditions. As Nagarjuna says in his text called *Fundamental Wisdom*,

> For whichever (system) emptiness is possible
> For that all is possible
> For whichever (system) emptiness is not possible
> For that nothing is possible

The meaning of emptiness is being empty of inherent existence and that means being dependent on something else, being dependent on causes and conditions. When we say something is dependent on other phenomena, it means that when those phenomena change, that particular thing will also change. If it were not dependent on something else and had inherent existence, then it would not be subject to change due to other conditions.

So, during the second turning of the wheel of doctrine, teaching that phenomena lack inherent existence, the Buddha taught clearly that phenomena can be made to change, because they are dependent on causes and conditions. Now although phenomena lack inherent existence when they appear to us, we think that they exist inherently. Not only do phenomena appear as if they are inherently existent, but we also become attached to them and determine that they exist inherently. In this way, we generate craving, desire, anger and so forth. When we encounter some pleasant or interesting object, we generate a lot of attachment and if we see something distasteful or unappealing, we get angry. Therefore problems like anger and attachment arise because of conceiving phenomena as inherently existent.

The conception of phenomena as inherently existent is a wrong consciousness mistaken towards its referent object, which provides the foundation for all delusions. However, if we generate an understanding that phenomena are not inherently existent, it will act as a counter force to that wrong consciousness. This shows that the defilements of the mind can be removed. If the delusions which defile the mind are removable then the seeds or potencies left behind by these delusions can also be eliminated. The total purity of the nature of the mind, which is its lack of inherent existence, is taught very explicitly in the second turning of the wheel of the doctrine. During the third turning of the wheel, it is explained again not only from the ultimate, but also from the conventional point of view, that the ultimate nature of the mind is pure, and in its pure state it is only neutral and clear light.

For example, whoever we are, delusions do not manifest within us all the time. What is more, even towards the same object we sometimes generate anger, sometimes generate love, which ought not be possible if things have inherent existence. This clearly shows that the real nature of the principal mind, the mind itself, is pure, but due to mental factors or the minds that accompany the principal mind, it sometimes appears to have a virtuous quality like love, and at others appears to have virtuous quality like love, and at others it appears in a deluded form like anger. That the nature of the principal mind is therefore neutral, but being dependent on its accompanying mind it may change from a virtuous to a non-virtuous mind.

So, the mind by nature is clear light and the defilements or delusions are temporary and adventitious. This indicates that if we practice and cultivate virtuous qualities, the mind can be transformed positively. On the other hand, if it encounters delusions then it will take on the form of delusions. Therefore all such qualities as the ten powers of the Buddha can also be attained because of this quality of the mind.

For example, all the different kinds of consciousness have the same quality of understanding and knowing their object clearly, but when a particular consciousness encounters some obstacle it is not able to understand its object. Although my eye consciousness has the potential to see an object, if I cover it up it will be obstructed from seeing the object. Similarly, the consciousness may not be able to see the object because it is too far away. So the mind already has the potential to understand all phenomena, a quality that need not be strengthened, but it may be obstructed by other factors.

With the attainment of the higher qualities of a Buddha, like the ten powers, we attain a full state of consciousness able to see the object very clearly and completely. This too can be attained merely by recognising the real nature of the mind and removing the delusions and obstructions from it.

During the third turning of the wheel of the doctrine, of the four noble truths initially taught during the first turning of the wheel, the meaning of the true path is explained very clearly by defining the meaning of *tathagatagarbha*, or Buddha nature. This makes possible the attainment of omniscience, the ultimate state of consciousness able to see phenomena and their ultimate mode of being.

Therefore, a complete explanation of the meaning of the true cessation is given during the second turning of the wheel of the doctrine and very detailed explanation of the true path is given during the third turning of the wheel. It explains the mind's potential to know phenomena's ultimate mode of existence and how omniscience can be achieved if you promote and develop that.

Now, when it comes to explaining the ultimate nature of the mind and its suitability for attaining enlightenment, we have the accounts of both sutra and tantra. These are differentiated by the details of their explanation of the nature of the mind. The tantric teachings give a very clear explanation of the subtlest state of enlightenment within the highest class of tantra, that is Highest Yoga Tantra. The first three classes of the tantra form a foundation for that.

In essence, this is a brief explanation of the Buddha's teaching, from the Four Noble Truths up to the highest class of tantric teaching. However, even if we have a clear understanding of the ultimate nature of the mind and the possibility of attaining enlightenment with it, if we do not practise and make effort to achieve that goal, then enlightenment will not be attainable. So while on the one hand it is important to know the ultimate nature of the mind, on the other, we should generate an intention to practise and realise this potential.

In teaching the first two Noble Truths the Buddha described the faults, the defects that must be given up and eliminated, that is true suffering and the true origin of suffering. In teaching the second pair of the Four Noble Truths, that is the true path and true cessation, the Buddha explained that there is a method, a path to get rid of these sufferings and delusions through which the complete cessation of those delusions can be attained. If there were no cure or method to eliminate suffering and attain a state of complete cessation and peace, it would not be necessary to discuss, think about or meditate on suffering, because it would merely engender pessimism and create more suffering for yourself. It would be better to remain bewildered and carefree. However, in fact we do have a chance, there is path and method to get rid of suffering, so it is worthwhile to talk and think about suffering. This is the importance and encompassing quality of the Buddha's teaching of the Four Noble Truths, for they provide the basis and foundation of all practices.

When we think about suffering and the true origin of suffering, and we come to an understanding of these two truths, we will generate a wish to rid ourselves of the suffering and its causes. In other words, because we dislike true suffering and the true origin of suffering we will generate a wish to reject them. This is called the determination to be free.

When you carefully consider suffering, it is not only you who are under its power, for other sentient beings also suffer in the same way. Then you should think that as other sentient beings are suffering just like me, how marvellous it would be if they could also eliminate suffering and its causes. Such a wish for other sentient beings to eliminate the suffering and its causes is called compassion. When, induced by compassion, you decide that you will help them yourself to eliminate suffering and its causes, that is the special resolve or the mind that wishes actively to benefit other sentient beings.

Then, if you look carefully at how sentient beings can be benefitted not just temporarily but ultimately, you will come to the conclusion that you will only be able to benefit them completely if you help them attain enlightenment and to do that, you must attain enlightenment yourself. This compassionate mind wishing to attain Buddhahood in order to help all sentient beings attain enlightenment is called the mind of enlightenment.

It is feasible to get rid of suffering and attain the ultimate status of enlightenment because phenomena do not have independent or inherent existence. Therefore it is important to understand the nature of phenomena, their lack of inherent existence. This understanding of phenomena's lack of inherent existence is called right view.

It is these three qualities: the determination to be free, mind of enlightenment, and right or correct view which are treated here as the three principal paths. They are so-called because they provide the real motivation for attaining liberation from cyclic existence and form the framework for attaining enlightenment.

The principal means of attaining liberation from cyclic existence is the determination to be free and the principal means of attaining enlightenment is the mind of enlightenment. Both of these are augmented by the right view or wisdom realising emptiness.

Now I will begin to explain the text.

The Homage

I pay homage to the foremost venerable lamas

This line is the author's expression of respect before composing the text. I will explain the meaning of some of the words here. The term lama denotes not only a position of status and power in the mundane sense, but rather indicates someone who is truly kind and possesses immense qualities. The Tibetan word *Jey* or foremost here signifies someone who cares less about the immediate or sensual pleasures of this world, this life in cyclic existence than for the next life. It refers to someone who is more concerned about other sentient beings' long term benefit over many lives to come. The Tibetan word *tsun*, meaning venerable or disciplined, refers to the lama because he has understood that, however pleasing or attractive they might be, the pleasures and attractions of cyclic existence are worthless. He has seen the lack of any lasting value among worldly phenomena, and has turned his mind towards the longer lasting happiness of future lives. In other words, the lama is one who has disciplined his mind and is not hankering after the delights of this world but aspires for the attainment of liberation. The word *lama* actually means supreme, indicating one who has greater care for other sentient beings than for himself and neglects his own interests for their sake.

'I pay homage', implies bowing down. You bow down to the lama on seeing his quality of concern for other sentient beings and their happiness at the cost of his own. In paying respect to this quality in the lama, by bowing down to him, you make an aspiration to attain such qualities yourself.

The Promise to Compose the Text

I will explain, as well as I can,
The essence of all the teachings of the Conqueror,
The path praised by the Conqueror's Children,
The entrance for the fortunate desiring liberation.

The first line expresses the author's promise to compose the text. The second implies the determination to be free, because all the Buddha's teachings are aimed towards liberation. It is from this point of view, the aim of attaining liberation, that we should be able to see faults in the attractions of cyclic existence and generate a wish to renounce them. This is actually imperative if we wish to achieve liberation. So this line implies renunciation of cyclic existence.

The words, 'Conqueror's Children' in the third line have three connotations. They can refer to those born from the Buddha's body, speech, or mind. Rahula was his physical son. The offspring of his speech refers to the Hearers and Solitary Buddhas. But in this context the 'Conqueror's Children' refers to those born from the mind of the Buddha, those who have generated the mind of enlightenment. You become a Bodhisattva or child of the Buddha only if you have this altruistic aspiration for enlightenment. Bodhisattvas are called offspring of the Buddha's mind, because they are born from qualities found in the mindstream of the Buddhas.

The last line of the verse implies right view, as the attainment of liberation is dependent on whether you have realised emptiness. So, these three lines summaries the meaning of the determination to be free, the mind of enlightenment, and view of emptiness that are explained in this text.

Exhorting the Disciples to Listen

Those who are not attached to the joys of the cyclic existence
Strive to make meaning of this leisure and opportunity,
Rely on the path pleasing to the Conqueror;
Those fortunate ones, listen with a clear mind.

Most of us here have sufficient resources so we do not have to work
very much to obtain food, clothing and so forth. But it is clear that in
this life merely having something to wear and something to eat is not
enough. We want something else. We still yearn for something more.
This clearly illustrates that unless pleasure and happiness are brought
about through transforming the mind, it is not possible to achieve
lasting happiness through external means, however favourable the
external conditions may be. Happiness and discomfort are very much
dependent on our mental attitude. So it is important that we should
bring about some internal transformation of the mind. Since lasting
happiness can only be attained in this way it is important to rely on
the power of mind and to discover the mind's ultimate nature.

There are many diverse teachings in different religious traditions
on how to bring about such a transformation. The Buddha's teaching,
which we are discussing here contains a very clear, detailed and
systematic explanation.

We do more or less qualify as 'fortunate ones' as referred to in this
verse, because we are trying to reduce our attachment, we are trying
to make meaningful use of this precious life as a free and fortunate
human being, and we are relying on the teachings of the Buddha. So,
this line tells us to pay attention to the teaching that the author is
going to impart.

Need to Generate the Determination to be Free

Without a pure determination to be free, there is no means to
  achieve peace
Due to fixation upon the pleasurable effects of the ocean of existence.
Embodied beings are thoroughly bound by craving for existence,
Therefore, in the beginning seek a determination to be free.

Here we begin the actual body of the text, the actual teaching it
contains. This verse explains the necessity of generating a determination
to be free or a mind seeking a release from cyclic existence. Seeing the
faults and shortcomings of cyclic existence and generating a very strong
wish to abandon it and attain liberation is called a determination to
be free. As long as you are unable to see worthlessness of the pleasures
of the cyclic existence, but continue to see some meaning or attraction
in them and cling to them, you will neither be able to turn your mind
towards liberation and nor will you realise how you are bound.

So the first line of this verse says that unless you have a pure
determination to free yourself from the ocean of cyclic existence, your
attempts to achieve peace will be in vain. It is our fascination with
cyclic existence due to craving and attachment, that binds us within
it. Therefore, if we really seek the peace of liberation, the right course
to adopt is to generate the determination to be free, to recognise the
faults of cyclic existence and reject them. The biography of Buddha
himself can provide us a clear understanding of the meaning of the
determination to be free for our own practice.

He was born a prince in a wealthy family, was well educated, had
a wife and son and enjoyed all imaginable worldly pleasures. Yet, despite
all the alluring pleasures available to him, when he came across
examples of the sufferings of birth, sickness, old age, and death, he
was provoked by the sight of others' suffering. He discovered for himself
that, no matter how attractive external comforts may be, so long as
you have a physical body like ours, which is the short-lived product of

contaminated action and delusion, then such attractive external pleasures are illusory. Understanding this, he tried to find a path to liberation from suffering and renounced all worldly pleasures, including his wife and son. Through gradually increasing his determination to be free in this way he was able to attain not only liberation, but also enlightenment.

Therefore it is taught that we need to develop a determination to free. Merely renouncing the comforts of cyclic existence and checking attachment and craving towards it is not enough. We must cut the stream of births. Rebirth comes about due to craving and desire, and we must cut its continuity through the practice of meditation. Hence, the Buddha entered into deep meditative stabilisation for six years. Finally by means of a union of calm abiding and special insight he attained the power to overcome the hindrances presented by the aggregates and external evil forces. He eliminated the very source of disturbing emotions and because they were extinguished he also overcame death. In this way he conquered all four evil forces or hindrances.

As followers of the Buddha, we too should try to see faults in the alluring attractions of cyclic existence. Then without attachments towards them generate concentration and focus on the view of selflessness-understanding the real nature of phenomena.

Now, should you wonder how to practise this determination to be free, how to generate a mind that wishes to renounce cyclic existence, the next verse says:

> Contemplating how freedom and fortune are difficult to find
> And that in life there is no time to waste, blocks the attraction to
>   captivating appearances of this life.
> Repeatedly contemplating actions' infallible effects
> And the sufferings of cyclic existence, blocks the captivating
>   appearance of future lives.

This verse explains how to check attachment first to this life and then towards future lives. In order to cut attachment towards the pleasures of this life, it is important to think about the preciousness of this human life, how it is difficult to find and the many qualities it provides. If we think clearly about these points, we will be able to extract meaning from having attained a human birth. Life as a human being is precious because with it we attain a status, quality and intelligence, which is absent in all other animals, even in all other sentient beings. We have the power to achieve great benefit and destruction. If we were to just while away our time and waste this precious potential in silly and meaningless activities, it would be a great loss.

Therefore, it is important that we recognise our capacity, our qualities and supreme intelligence which other sentient beings do not possess. If we can identify these things, we will be able to appreciate and use them. The power of the human brain and human intelligence is marvellous. It is capable of planning ahead and can engage in deep and extensive thought, as other sentient beings cannot. Since we have such a powerful brain or intelligence, it is very important that we first recognise the strength and character of this awareness. We should then steer it in the right direction, so that it can contribute significantly to peace and harmony in the world and within all sentient beings.

Let us take the example of nuclear energy. There is great power within a nuclear particle, but if we use that power wrongly or mishandle it, it can be very destructive. Nowadays we have nuclear missiles and other weapons the very names of which make us afraid, because they are so destructive. They can cause mass destruction in a fraction of time. On the other hand, if we put nuclear power to use in a constructive way, it can be of great service to humanity and sentient beings at large. Similarly, since human beings have such capacity and power, it is very important that they use it for the benefit of all sentient beings. Properly employed human ingenuity can be a great source of benefit and happiness, but if misused it can bring great misery and destruction.

It is from the point of view of this keen intelligence that we should think about the significance of our precious human life. However, it is also important to understand that the life of a free and fortunate human being is not only meaningful and difficult to find, but it is also short-lived.

The next two lines say that if we think repeatedly about the infallible connection between causes, our actions, and the sufferings of cyclic existence, we will be able to cut our attachment to the next life. At present we engage in many levels of activity to obtain clothing, food and a good name. In addition, our experiences in the latter part of our lives are dependent on the actions that we have performed in the earlier part. This actually is the meaning of actions and results. Although it is not the subtlest interpretation, when we talk about actions and results, actions includes any of the things we do in order to obtain any kind of happiness or pleasure. The results are the effects that we achieve thereby. Therefore, in the first part of our lives we engage in certain kinds of activity that we think will lead to some kind of happiness or success in the future. Similarly, we engage in certain kinds of action in this life so that we may be able to achie good result in our next life. In other words, our experiences in the latter part of our lives are dependent on the actions we have performed in the earlier part of our lives and our experiences in the future lives, whether pleasant or unpleasant, are dependent on the actions that we have committed in former lives.

These actions are done by either body, speech or mind and so are termed physical, verbal and mental actions. From the point view of the result that they produce, they can be termed wholesome, unwholesome or neutral actions. Wholesome actions give rise to pleasant results, unwholesome actions give rise to unpleasant results and neutral actions lead to a feeling of equanimity. Then there are actions that will definitely give rise to a result and those that will not. For example, when an action comes into being, it is motivated, there is an intention, then it is actually implemented and finally it is brought to a conclusion.

Now, when the intention, action and conclusion are all very strong, it is definite that the action will give rise to a result, whether good or bad. On the other hand, if the intention is very strong but you do not put it into effect, or if at the end instead of thinking that you have completed the deed, you regret what you have done, then that particular action may not produce an effect at that time. If these three aspects intention, application and conclusion, are not present the action is classified as indefinite. From the point of view of the basis experiencing the result, there are actions that give fruit in this very life, actions that give fruit in the immediate next life, actions whose fruits will be experienced in many lives after the next.

Then there are two levels of action which can be classified as projecting and completing actions. Projecting actions are those actions which are responsible for projecting us into a particular life through birth as a human being, animal or other state of being. Completing actions are those that determine the quality of whatever life you are born into. For example, despite being a human being you may be perpetually poor. Right from birth your sense faculties may be damaged or your limbs crippled. On the other hand, your complexion may be radiant and you may have a natural strength. Even born as an animal you might, like a pet dog, have a comfortable home. These kinds of qualities or defects that you inherit right from birth, are the results of completing actions. So a particular action can be termed projecting or completing according to their function. It is possible that although the projecting actions is wholesome, the completing action is non-virtuous, and that although the completing actions is unwholesome, the projecting action is virtuous.

Whether a particular action is positive, like faith in the Buddha, or negative, like attachment, if in its own terms it is pure, it can be seen as completely white and virtuous or completely black and unwholesome. If the preparation, application and conclusion of a particular action are totally virtuous then that action can be seen as a virtuous action. But if it results from impure preparation, application and conclusion, then it can be seen as an unwholesome action. If it is a result of a mixed intention, pure application and impure conclusion, in other words, if it is a mixture of both positive and negative qualities, then it can be called a mixed action.

It is the 'I', or the person, who accumulates an action and experiences its results. Although these different levels of actions, are the product of the thinking of particular sentient beings, they are not produced by a creator of the world. There is someone who creates the action, because when we talk about action, the world itself clearly implies that there is an actor or agent who performs that action but it is not an external agent.

How does an action give rise to a result? For example, when I snap my fingers, immediately I stop, the action is a complete, leaving behind a result. If you ask, what that result is, it is the mere disintegration of the action, and the disintegration of an action goes on continuously. So when we talk about the result of a particular action, it is the mere disintegration or part of the disintegration, or the cessation of that particular action. To clarify the point it is a kind of potency left behind by the disintegration of that action, which is responsible for bringing forth many other conditioned phenomena.

If you wonder where the imprints of that potency of the disintegration or cessation of that particular action is left, the answer is on the continuum of the consciousness existing during the immediate moment of the cessation of the action. There are occasions when the consciousness is alert and awake and there are occasions when the consciousness is latent, for example, when we are in deep sleep, or when we faint. Therefore, the consciousness is not a wholly reliable place to deposit such a potency. Sometimes it is very subtle and sometimes it is very coarse, so the consciousness provides only temporary basis for such imprints.

Hence, if we seek an ultimate explanation, it is the mere 'I', or the person, which carries the potency of a particular action. This explanation is based on the ultimate explanation of the highest school, that is the Middle Way Consequentialist School. I used the word 'mere I' to clarify that the 'I' or the person has only nominal not inherent existence. It is only designated and does not exist by itself. It is not something that you can point at with your finger. The word 'mere' indicates an 'I' which is merely designated by name and thought and negates a self-supporting or independent 'I'. The negation of an inherently existent or self-supporting 'I' does not mean that 'I' or person becomes the basis on which the imprint or potency of an action is left. In general, the 'I' is designated to the collection of physical and mental aggregates.

When we talk about the physical body and the consciousness, which is the basis of designation of the 'I', with reference to a human being, it is principally the consciousness which becomes the basis of designation of the term 'I'. The consciousness has many levels, some of them coarse and some of them subtle. The physical body of a human being can also be divided into many parts, such as the eye, the ear, and so forth. These physical parts again become a basis for the designation of consciousness. For example, the eye consciousness is designated to the eye, the ear consciousness to the ear and so forth. But if you try to find the subtlest basis of designation of consciousness,

it seems that the nerves and pathways of the brain
basis of designation of mental consciousness. Then the.
of the bases of the sense powers and these are supposed to
subtle. It is not clear whether such bases of the sense faculties can
found in the brain or somewhere else. It will be an interesting object
of research.

Let us take an example, in order to generate an eye consciousness
many conditions or causes are necessary. The dominant cause is an
undefective eye sense power. Having a particular form within its focus
becomes the objective condition. However, despite the presence of
such conditions it is not definite that an eye consciousness will arise.
This indicates that a third condition, the immediately preceding
condition, which is a consciousness, is required in addition to the
external objective condition and internal dominant condition of a
sense power. Therefore, in order for the eye sense consciousness to
arise all three conditions are necessary.

As an example to elucidate this point, there are occasionally cases
of people who after a long illness become so physically weak that their
heartbeat and all physical functions stop. Entering into such a deep
coma that no physical activity or function can be perceived, the doctor
declares them clinically dead. However, sometimes after a few minutes
or even hours, despite the apparent lack of physical activity, the person
starts breathing again, the heart starts beating, and physical functions
are regained. This revival, despite the previous cessation of all physical
functions, shows the unavoidable presence of a mental condition that
immediately preceded it. When that immediately preceding condition,
a consciousness, is present the person can come back to life again.
Similarly, in the case of a sense consciousness the mere presence of the
dominant condition and the objective condition is not sufficient to
generate a particular consciousness.

According to the Buddhist view, when we talk about the various
levels of consciousness of a particular human being which are
designated to the various parts of his body then we are referring to the
coarser levels of consciousness of a person. These consciousness are
called consciousness of a human being because they are dependent on
particular parts of a human body. Therefore, when a human being
dies, all the coarser levels of consciousness that are dependent on the

physical body also seem to disappear, but it is interesting to note that their arising as entities of consciousness does not come about merely due to the presence of the physical body. They are produced as entities of clarity and awareness such as eye conciseness, ear consciousness and so forth, in dependence on conditions other than the body. There is a fundamental cause that generates these consciousness as entities of clarity and awareness and according to the various conditions it encounters consciousnesses cognizing form, sound and so forth arise. This shows that there is a consciousness independent of the coarser physical body, but when it encounters coarse conditions, it appears in the form of consciousness.

Consciousness has a much subtler nature and if you examine that subtler nature, then the real, substantial cause of that consciousness can only be another continuum of consciousness which preceded it, irrespective of whether there is a physical body or not. Therefore, there is plainly a kind of innate natural mind, which is totally pure and clear. When this pure state of the mind comes into contact with different levels of physical body, consciousness also manifests itself more or less coarsely, depending upon what particular physical body it is being designated to. But if you examine the real nature of the mind, it has an existence independent of the coarser levels of the physical body.

Such a pure, natural state of mind, which exists independently of the physical body, is called primordial clear light or the primordial consciousness - a consciousness which has always been present. Compared to this, coarser consciousness are adventitious, because they are sometimes present and at other times absent. This primordial innate clear light consciousness is the real basis of designation of a sentient being or person So, whoever has this kind of consciousness, this pure state of the mind, is termed a sentient being and this is the main criterion that differentiates sentient beings from other living things and other phenomena. No doubt a person or 'I' is attributed to the total aggregate of the physical body and the consciousness, but it is the primordial innate clear light that is the exclusive basis of designation of a person, and not the physical body. Even plants and flowers have a kind of physical body, but since they lack this kind of innate subtle consciousness they are not referred to as persons. Whatever your shape, form or outer aspect, anyone who possesses a continuity of consciousness and has feelings, perception and so on is referred to as a person. Therefore different texts explain that the 'I' or the person has been attributed to the continuity or stream of consciousness.

Although specific consciousness vary according to different occasions and coarser levels of consciousness are dependent upon various physical bodies, the subtlest level of consciousness, the mere entity of clarity and awareness, the primordial innate clear light consciousness, is independent of the physical body. The nature of consciousness has no beginning. If you try to trace the origin of consciousness, you can go further and further back but you will not reach a point at which you can say, this is where this consciousness came into being. Therefore, it is a kind of natural law that consciousness came into existence from beginningless time.

This is also a more realistic explanation, because if you accept a beginning of consciousness, you either have to assert a creator of consciousness or you have to say that consciousness arises without any cause. This is preposterous, out of concern for which consciousness has been explained as beginningless. If you ask why it is beginningless, we can only say that it is a natural law. If we observe carefully, there are so many things in this world whose continuity can be traced from beginningless time. But if you ask, what is their real and ultimate origin, you can find no answer. This is simply their nature. If you ask why physical forms appear in the entity of form, it is simply due to their nature. If we say that this comes about without cause or from unrelated causes, why can it not occur causelessly now, when it could previously occur without cause?

Therefore according to the Buddhist view, if you ask whether there is a beginning to consciousness, the answer is that the continuum of consciousness is beginningless, the origin of the 'I' or the person is beginningless and birth is beginningless. And if you ask whether these things have an end, again the answer is negative if you are thinking about the mere continuum of consciousness or the mere continuum of a person. But there is an end to the impure state of mind, the impure state of a person and there is also a limit to birth, because normally when we talk about birth, we are referring to something which has been produced through contaminated action and delusion.

So because of the beginninglessness of birth, later experiences of suffering and pleasure are connected to actions performed earlier. The different kinds of deluded actions or virtuous actions that a person accumulates in different lives are connected to results in different lives. For example, if you commit some virtuous or negative actions in this life, then you will have to experience their results later on. Similarly, you may have committed some virtuous or unwholesome actions in a past life, whose results you will have to experience in that very life, or in this life. If you have not accumulated such actions, then you will never experience their effects. On the other hand, if you have accumulated a particular action, then generally speaking you will never escape the result: sooner or later it will bear fruit. Similarly if one has accumulated a positive action the result will be definitely positive. Those kinds of actions are called definite actions, but there are also actions whose result is not very definite, because the proper conditions or situations were not present. Furthermore there are actions, which seem of minor importance, but whose results multiply rapidly depending upon the circumstances, situation and conditions. So, there are many kinds of action: definite action, indefinite action, actions that multiply greatly, as well as the fact that the results of actions not done will not be encountered and that actions once done will not dissipate.

Usually, all our daily actions arise from some wish or desire. For example, if you wish to go somewhere, then you actually set out and go; if you wish to eat something then you look for something to eat and eat it. Desire can be classified into two types, one which is negative and another which is logical and creative. For example, the wish to attain liberation from cyclic existence results in a reasonable undertaking, therefore it is a sound and logical desire. On the other hand, to generate attachment towards a particular object, such that you wish to obtain or achieve something, is an impure desire and usually arises from a misconception of phenomena as existing independently or inherently. Most of the work that we do in cyclic existence, and the desires that we generate, are the results of this kind of illogical reasoning.

Familiarising our minds with positive qualities and trying to achieve goals like liberation are logical desires. Still, it is possible that in particular cases an individual's wish to attain liberation is assisted by the conception of true existence. However, every wish for worldly perfection is based on the ignorance that conceives of true existence. On these grounds it is better to classify desire in two ways, one the result of correct reasoning and the other the result of incorrect reasoning.

The result of desire based on the conception of the true existence is cyclic existence. Still, there is another kind of desire based on sound reasoning that does not project cyclic existence, but aspires to attain the supreme attainments and qualities of the Buddha, the Doctrine, the Spiritual Community and Nirvana, the state beyond suffering. There is a wish and desire to attain them.

If we do not classify desire into two types as mentioned above, we might think that desiring liberation was improper, that desiring religious practice was improper and that even wishing for happiness was also improper. No doubt there are different modes of desiring your own happiness, but what is clear is that so long as we have attachment and a conception of a truly existent self those actions characteristic of cyclic existence will continue to be created.

Generally speaking, once an action has been accumulated the result has to be experienced. Therefore, although we may be enjoying the delights of cyclic existence just now and intense sufferings are not manifest, since we are not free from the actions' schackles and snares we have no security and no guarantee of lasting happiness. This is the perspective from which this particular text says,

> If you think repeatedly about the infallible law of actions and results.
> And the sufferings of cyclic existence,
> You will be able to stop attachment to the next life.

By understanding the infallible law of actions and results you will be able to see that unless you completely purify your actions, whatever kind of apparent enjoyment and pleasure you find in cyclic existence will be unreliable. Having understood this, you will not be confused by the pleasures of cyclic existence and will be able to curb your attachment to the next life.

As a human being in cyclic existence we normally encountered four kinds of suffering: the sufferings of birth, old age, sickness, and death. Right from birth, we are faced with sufferings; our life begins with suffering. At the same time the process of ageing begins and we start to encounter different degrees of sickness. Even when we are healthy we encounter a lot of disturbances and confusion. Finally, the chapter of our life is closed with the sufferings of death.

When we talk about someone who is in cyclic existence, we are referring to a sentient being who is uncontrollably under the sway of contaminated actions and delusions. Because we are overpowered by contaminated actions and delusions, we repeatedly have to take birth in a cycle, therefore it is called cyclic existence. Of the two, contaminated actions and delusion, it is delusions which are mainly responsible for casting us into cyclic existence. When we are free of delusions we attain liberation. Delusions are states of mind which, when they arise within our mental continuums, leave us disturbed, confused and unhappy. Therefore, those states of mind, which delude or afflict us are called delusions or afflictive emotions. They are the negative qualities which make us unhappy when they arise within us. It is these internal disturbances and not external conditions that really make us suffer.

As long as we have those evildoers residing within us happiness is impossible. So, if we really want to transform ourselves and achieve maximum happiness, we must identify these deluded states of mind and eliminate them. Enlightenment, the state of greatest happiness, cannot be actualised by any other means than by transforming our minds. Usually on an ordinary level, we think of delusions like attachment and anger as qualities that make life meaningful and colourful. We think that without attachment and anger our whole society or community would become colourless and without life. But if you think carefully about it and weigh up the qualities and disadvantages of delusions like attachment and anger, you may find that in the short term they give you some relief and make your life colourful. But on closer scrutiny you will find that the fewer of these delusions we have, even though life may be less colourful, the more we will develop inner calm, inner strength and lasting happiness. Consequently, our minds will be happy, our physical health will improve and we will be able to engage successfully in virtuous activities.

Of course, you might feel that your life now is colourless, unattractive and without meaning. But if you think carefully and look for your own and other sentient beings' long term benefit, you will notice that the more you control your delusions, the greater your peace of mind and physical well-being. In pursuit of physical health, many people do various kind of yoga exercises. No doubt this is very good for them, but if they were also to do some mental yoga that would be even better. In short, as long as your mind is disturbed and unsound, you will continue to encounter problems and sufferings. And as long as your mind is under control, disciplined and free from these faults, the more you will gain inner strength, calm, peace and stability, due to which you will be able to be more creative. From our own experience that we have more suffering when our minds are more disturbed by faults we can deduce that when our minds are completely clear our experience of happiness will be stable.

Up to this point we have been discussing the faults, sufferings and delusions of cyclic existence. On the one hand, we have to think about the faults and sufferings of cyclic existence and generate aversion to them and on the other we need to ascertain the possibility of attaining nirvana, the cessation of suffering - the complete elimination of delusions. If you were to ask - is there really a method by which we can attain liberation, or a method by which we will be able to eliminate sufferings and delusions completely? It would be worthwhile asking whether nirvana or liberation actually exists.

Liberation or cessation is the nature of the mind on the occasion of the complete annihilation of defilements by their antidotes. When you think about the sufferings of cyclic existence and you are weary of them, you look forward to nirvana, liberation, as an alternative. Let us say that we have a defiled and deluded mind. When the defilements of the previous moment of the continuum of this particular consciousness are completely eliminated, the very nature of that purified consciousness is liberation, nirvana or true cessation. In other words, the teachings say that the cyclic existence that we are presently experiencing is not eternal, because it has arisen from causes and conditions and they can be counteracted.

If you ask what the cause of cyclic existence is: it is ignorance, the conception of true existence. And what is the remedy for such ignorance? It is the wisdom realising emptiness or wisdom realising the real nature of phenomena. Now, these two qualities, ignorance, which is the cause of cyclic existence, and the wisdom realising emptiness, which is the antidote to ignorance, cannot abide simultaneously in the continuum of one human being because they are mutually exclusive. Although both observe the same object, their modes of apprehension are completely opposed to each other. Therefore, they cannot both abide in one person's continuum with equal strength. As one is strengthened the other is weakened.

If you examine these two qualities carefully, you will find that whereas ignorance has no valid support or foundation, the wisdom realising emptiness does. Any quality that has a valid foundation can be strengthened and developed limitlessly. On the other hand, because the conception of true existence lacks a valid foundation, when it encounters the wisdom realising emptiness, a valid mind based on correct reasoning, it is weakened such that it can finally be eliminated altogether. So, ultimately, the wisdom realising the nature of phenomena will be able to uproot ignorance, the source of cyclic existence.

If we examine how attachment and anger arise within us when our minds are calm and clear, in what way we crave the object, how it appears to us and how we generate a conception of true existence towards it, we will be able to see how these delusions arise within us. Although we may not gain a direct understanding, we can make some correct assumptions.

How are attachment and anger supported by the conception of true existence? When, for example, you are very angry with somebody, notice how at that time you see that person as completely obnoxious, completely unpleasant. Then, later a friend tells you, no that person is not completely unpleasant because he has this or that quality. Just hearing these words, you change your mind and no longer see the person you were angry with as completely obnoxious and unpleasant. This clearly shows that right from the beginning, when you generate attachment, anger and so forth, the mental tendency is to see that particular person or object not as merely pleasant or unpleasant, but as completely unpleasant or completely pleasant. If the person is pleasant you see him or her as completely attractive, one hundred percent attractive and if you are angry with them, you see that person as completely unattractive. In other words, you see whatever quality they have as existing inherently or independently. Therefore, this mode of apprehending phenomena as existing inherently or truly provides a strong basis for the arising of delusions like attachment and anger.

From such explanations you can make an assumption that in general this quality, liberation or nirvana, does exist. It is a phenomenon. Not only does it exist, but it is something that you can achieve within your mental continuum. If you train yourself in the twin practices of thinking about the disadvantages and sufferings of cyclic existence, and the advantages of being able to get rid of these sufferings and the possibility of attaining liberation then you will be able to generate a determination to become completely free from cyclic existence.

The Measure of Having Generated a Determination to be Free

The next verse explains how to gauge whether you have generated a determination to be free of cyclic existence:

> Having familiarised ourself in this way, if you do not generate admiration
> For the prosperity of cyclic existence even for an instant,
> And if you wish for liberation day and night,
> At that time you have generated the determination to be free.

The next verses explain the generation of the mind of enlightenment. First the need and purpose of generating altruism is explained.

The Purpose of Generating the Mind of Enlightenment

> If this determination to be free is not influenced by a pure mind of
> enlightenment
> It will not become a cause for unsurpassable enlightenment, the
> perfect bliss.
> Therefore, the intelligent should generate a mind of enlightenment.

However strong your familiarity with the determination to be free of cyclic existence may be, unless you generate an altruistic attitude, a strong wish to benefit sentient beings, it will be impossible for you to attain enlightenment. In this regard Nagarjuna's *Precious Garland* says:

> If you and this world wish
> To actualise supreme enlightenment
> Its root is the mind of enlightenment.

The basis for generating an altruistic aspiration for enlightenment is compassion, of which there are many types. One kind of compassion is to think how nice it would be if sentient beings were free from suffering. There are other degrees of compassion which include not only this thought, but also have greater courage. This induces a special resolve to take responsibility personally for getting rid of sentient beings' sufferings. Even the Hearers and Solitary Buddhas strongly wish that sentient beings be separated from suffering. Similarly, we ourselves sometimes generate the kind of compassion which thinks how nice it would be if sentient beings were free from sufferings. For example, seeing the misery or neglected condition of a particular person or animal, we might generate a strong sense of compassion wishing that the sufferings of that particular sentient being be eliminated.

It is also important to note that when the object of our compassion is someone we like our sympathy is based on attachment rather than compassion. On the other hand, if seeing the sufferings of a neglected animal, such as a stray dog to whom you have no attachment at all, you generate compassion, that is pure compassion.

Now, the compassion generated by Hearers and Solitary Buddhas is of a much higher quality than the compassion we normally generate, because, seeing the suffering that pervades the whole of cyclic existence, they generate compassion for all sentient beings. Unable to see the sufferings of all cyclic existence, we see only the sufferings of particular beings, which we see only as some kind of fault or demerit in them. However, Hearers and Solitary Buddhas do not have a compassion that induces them to take responsibility for liberating sentient beings themselves.

The compassion generated by Bodhisattvas is of the highest kind. They not only wish that sentient beings be separated from suffering, but voluntarily take responsibility for adding them of their sufferings. This is called great compassion. It is this compassion which underlies the altruistic aspiration for enlightenment and which induces the special attitude. For this reason we often come across statements in the scriptures that it is compassion which acts as the root of the mind of enlightenment. In order to generate such compassion, on the one hand, you must identify the suffering by which the particular sentient being is afflicted. On the other hand you should regard that being as pleasant and dear to your heart.

The Means of Generating the Mind of Enlightenment

Carried away by the four torrential rivers
Bound by tight bonds of actions, difficult to undo,
Caught in the iron net of the conception of self
Thoroughly enveloped by the thick darkness of ignorance
Born into boundless cyclic existence,
And in their rebirths unceasing tormented by the three sufferings:
Contemplating the state of mother sentient beings in such
    conditions, generate the supreme mind

The words 'mother sentient beings' here clearly show that suffering sentient beings are not totally unrelated to you. They have acted as your mother in many previous lives and have been extremely kind to you. Therefore you should see them as very pleasing. Understanding how your mothers suffer will provoke in you a feeling of being unable to bear it. Through the mental process of recognising how you are intimately connected to sentient beings you will be able to generate the great compassion that gives rise to the mind of enlightenment. This verse says that sentient beings are being carried away by four torrential rivers. These four could refer to the four causes that project sentient beings into birth in cyclic existence and they could also refer to their four results. But, here, the four rivers refer to the four unwanted sufferings that we encounter in cyclic existence: that is birth, ageing, sickness and death. In other words, we are completely under the control of very strong, irreversible contaminated action, because of which we experience these four sufferings.

Such strongly contaminated actions also arise from potent delusions like anger and attachment. These in turn arise from a powerful conception of (a truly existent) self. This is compared to a strong iron net, due to which we are ensnared in cyclic existence. A strong conception of self means that it is stable and unchallenged. The stronger the conception of self is, the stronger delusions like anger and attachment will be. And the stronger the delusions are, the stronger the actions that project us into cyclic existence will be. And the stronger the actions that project us into cyclic existence are, the more powerful our sufferings will be.

The misconception of self arises because we are obscured on all sides by the darkness of ignorance. In this context the misconception of self that entraps us in cyclic existence actually refers to the misconception of self of persons, because the next line says that sentient beings are completely confused and enshrouded by the great darkness of ignorance. Usually the misconception of self itself is referred to as ignorance, but when we find two things explained, like the misconception of self and ignorance, the first, the misconception of self, refers to the misconception of self of persons, and ignorance in the next line refers to the misconception of self of phenomena, the misconception of phenomena as truly existent.

Our misconception of the true existence of phenomena, in other words our strong grasping for the attraction of our physical body, acts as the foundation for generating too much attachment towards our own person. Therefore, the misconception of phenomena acts as a foundation for the misconception of the person. When you observe the 'I' in your continuum and generate a feeling of 'I', a conception of a truly existent self, that is called the view of the transitory collection. So, the misconception of self of phenomena gives rise to this view of the transitory collection and this in turn stimulates the accumulation of action. And because of the misconception of self of phenomena and the misconception of self of persons, we involuntarily take birth in cyclic existence and for an immeasurable time experience an unceasing chain of suffering like birth, ageing, sickness and so forth.

Now, the cessation of subsequent results depends on the cessation of the preceding causes. If strong causes have been created then you have to experience their result, no matter how reluctant you are. If you think in this way, then the more you resent your sufferings the more you will loathe their causes. These verses explain two ways of generating renunciation and a determination to be free through thinking about true suffering. These are to think about the faults and sufferings of cyclic existence and to reflect on the true origins of suffering. When the verse explains the four levels of sufferings and so forth, it is explaining true suffering, and when it explains factors like the conception of true existence, ignorance and contaminated action, it is explaining the true origins of suffering. In this way, it explains the first two noble truths.

If you think about this cycle of suffering and its origins with reference to other sentient beings, it will lead to training in compassion. But if you think about these sufferings and their origins with reference to yourself it leads to generation of a determination to be free.

Yesterday we were discussing the different levels of suffering and how to generate an altruistic attitude wishing to benefit all sentient beings. In this context the text says:

> Seeing the sufferings of the mother sentient beings
> That are in such a situation we should generate the supreme mind.

In other words we must first observe the sufferings of the sentient beings and then generate a strong feeling of closeness and affection for them. The closer you feel to other sentient beings the easier it will be to generate feeling of being unable to bear their suffering. Therefore, we should view all sentient beings as our relatives, such as our mother.

In order to generate this mental attitude of concern for other sentient beings, we must first understand the beginningless nature of cyclic existence. The sentient beings who have taken birth in cyclic existence are also beginningless, therefore there is no sentient being who you can say has not been connected to you as a relative such as your mother.

In order to generate a strong sense of affection and closeness to all other sentient beings, you must first generate a strong sense of equanimity towards all sentient beings. Based on this feeling you can generate a sense of kinship with the rest of sentient beings and view them as your mother. Then, you will be able to reflect kindness of these sentient beings, which is the same as kindness of your present family which sustains you now. When you see them as your own relatives and remember their kindness you will be able to generate an attitude of cherishing them, taking them to your heart.

Another method of generating an altruistic attitude is to exchange yourself with others. This is possible because all other sentient beings are the same as you in wanting happiness and not wanting suffering. They are also same as you in having the capacity and the opportunity to get rid of suffering and attain happiness. Like you all sentient beings have the right to eliminate suffering and attain maximum happiness. Although you are the same from all these perspectives, all other sentient beings are countless. And yet you are not unrelated to them, because in worldly terms you are very much dependent on them. Even when you meditate on the path you do so by focusing on sentient beings. Finally ultimate enlightenment known as the effortless spontaneous achievement of others' purposes is achieved in dependence on them. Thus, we are related to and dependent on sentient beings when we are in cyclic existence, during the path and finally at the time of the fruit.

Now, seeing that you have this close connection with all other sentient beings, it is foolish to neglect their welfare to pursue the interests of only one being - yourself. On the other hand, it is wise to neglect the interests of one for the benefit of the rest who are the majority of sentient beings. All the pleasures and facilities that we enjoy in this life, such as wealth, possessions, fame and friendship, are all obtained in dependance on other beings. We cannot think of enjoying anything by our own efforts alone without their help. In this modern age especially, everything we enjoy, food, clothing and everything else, is produced by various manufacturing companies in which other people work. Almost nothing is grown or produced in your own small garden or courtyard.

We eat tinned fruit which is produced by the hands of other human beings. When we travel in an aeroplane, we depend on the work and facilities provided by the many people who are involved in running that aeroplane. In our modern society we cannot think of surviving without depending on other human beings. Equally, without other human beings you would have neither reputation nor fame. Even though you may have acquired certain qualities that are the basis of your fame and reputation, if other people do not know about them there is no question of your becoming famous.

If you think carefully, even your enemy, who you usually view as an opponent and completely dislike, gives you the chance to generate many qualities like patience, courage and strength. There is a teaching by Shantideva in his chapter on patience that is pertinent here about how to generate patience with respect to your enemy and regard him as precious. This is especially important for a Buddhist practitioner. If you are able to see how you can gain these kind of qualities from your enemy, you will also be able to generate kind feelings towards him.

If you are able to generate such a positive mind towards your enemy, who is normally an object of contempt, you will have no trouble in generating a feeling of care and concern towards neutral beings or of course to your friends. In order to generate such a mental attitude, it is not necessary that you recognise all the sentient beings individually. You can for example, infer that all trees have certain common characteristics from the qualities of one particular tree without having to know each and every individual tree. Similarly, you can conclude that all living beings are the same in wanting happiness and not wanting suffering, by examining your own situation. By doing so, you will easily generate compassion, which is an aspiration thinking how nice it would be if all sentient beings could eliminate suffering. If you are able to generate a clear understanding of the sufferings of sentient beings, you will also be able to generate love, which is to think how nice it would be if all sentient beings met with happiness.

Based on these two aspirations - love and compassion - you will generate the special attitude of taking responsibility for getting rid of these sufferings yourself and this will induce the mind that wishes to attain the highest enlightenment for the sake of all sentient beings. This altruistic aspiration for enlightenment for the sake of all sentient beings is called the mind of enlightenment. The way to measure your generation of the mind of enlightenment and determination to be free was explained earlier.

The Need to Realise Emptiness

From this point on the text explains the nature of emptiness and the wisdom that realises it. The first verse explains the need to generate this wisdom realising the nature of emptiness. There are various kinds of wisdom: wisdom understanding conventional phenomena such as the various sciences and wisdom understanding the ultimate, real nature of phenomena. If you do not possess wisdom realising the ultimate mode of existence, no matter how strong your determination to be free or your aspiration for enlightenment may be, you will not be able to shift the conception of true existence, the root cause of cyclic existence. Therefore, you should make an effort to realise dependent arising.

> Without the wisdom realising the mode of existence
> Even though you familiarise yourself with the determination to be
> free and the mind of enlightenment
> The root of cyclic existence cannot be cut.
> Therefore make an effort to realise dependent arising.

Common explanations of the meaning of dependent arising such as the dependent arising of cause and effect are accepted by all Buddhist traditions. But this verse refers to subtle dependent arising, something's coming into existence in dependence on its parts. In other words there are conditioned relations in which particular effects or phenomena arise merely in dependence on a particular cause and condition. Another meaning of dependent arising is the existence of things relative to others. For example, when we talk about the part of a whole body, we call it a part in relation to the whole, similarly the whole is only a whole in relation to its parts. From this point of view the part and whole are related to and dependent on each other. Likewise, qualities like long and short have a relative sense, because we use these terms to describe objects in relation to other objects.

At another level phenomena are also called dependent arising because they arise in dependence on their basis of designation and they are dependent on the mind that designates them. The first meaning of dependent arising applies only to conditioned phenomena, whereas the last two meanings apply to all phenomena, conditioned impermanent phenomena and unconditioned permanent phenomena.

The dependent arising referred to in this line is the subtlest one, in which it is explained in terms of existing merely by name and designation by thought. In other words when we say that phenomena exist through the power of terms and designations and in dependence on designations, we are explaining dependent arising as it appears, as mere existence due to the power of name. From the ultimate point of view that is mere emptiness of inherent existence. This means that since a phenomenon cannot come into being from its own side, it lacks inherent existence and is dependent on other conditions. Here other conditions refer to designation and the designating thought. The phenomenon exists merely by the power of that designation and as such it is empty of self-sufficient existence. Conversely, since it is empty of self-sufficient existence it exists through the power of designation.

So these are explanations of subtle emptiness. When we talk about the meaning of emptiness, we are talking about something being empty of its object of negation. Phenomena are empty of independent existence, inherent existence, and existence from their own side. These three: independent existence, inherent existence, existence from its own side are the objects of negation. Emptiness thus means being empty of these objects of negation. This is said because phenomena are dependent on something else, they are dependent on the name and the thought by which they are designated.

When we explain that they are dependent on their parts, name and designation, we are also stating that they do not have inherent existence, because dependence and independence are opposite terms. Phenomena are either dependent or independent, they cannot be both. Since these terms are mutually exclusive, a phenomenon can only be one or the other, it cannot be something in between. For example, human being and horse are opposites but not direct opposites, because there can be a third category, such as a dog, which is neither horse nor human being. But human being and non-human being are direct opposites and if we say that there are only two categories of phenomena, those that are either human being or non-human being, there cannot be a third category. So through the reasoning of depending arising, lack of inherent existence can be established.

When we use the term emptiness, it has some similarity to our usual idea of absence of something or voidness. But if you think that emptiness is the mere absence of anything, then your understanding is incomplete. We should understand emptiness as absence of inherent existence. Because they lack inherent existence, phenomena do not have an independent existence, yet they are existent. This understanding of emptiness can be gained through understanding the meaning of dependent arising, because dependent arising means that phenomena are dependent on something else. They do not exist independently nor do they exist from their own side. If phenomena exist in dependence on something else, this clearly shows that they do exist.

Sometimes emptiness is explained as the meaning of the middle way, which means the centre that has eliminated the two extremes. One extreme is to think that if phenomena do not exist inherently, they do not exist at all - the extreme of nihilism. The other is to think that if phenomena exist, they must exist inherently - the extreme of eternalism. If we have good understanding of emptiness, on the one hand we will understand that, since phenomena exist in dependence on thought and name and so on, they have nominal existence, that is they do exist. This avoids the extreme of nihilism. On the other hand, when you think about how phenomena exist in dependence on thought and name, it is clear that they do not have an independent existence. This avoids the extreme of eternalism. If it were something that did not exist at all, then to say that it depended on something else would not make any sense. The next verse clarifies this point.

> One who sees the infallible cause and effect
> Of all phenomena in cyclic existence and beyond
> And destroys all perceptions (of inherent existence)
> Has entered the path which pleases the Buddha

This means that if you are able to clearly assert the infallibility of dependent arising, such that you are able to generate an ascertainment of it, and if, without harming the presentation of dependent arising, you are able to destroy the perception that things exist inherently, then you have entered the path that pleases the Buddha. The fist two lines clearly explain that one who sees cause and effect, within and beyond cyclic existence, as infallible, who can posit the existence and actual function of cause and effect, rather than their nonexistence, is able to eliminate the extreme of nihilism. The next two lines explain that through understanding the function of cause and effect, you will understand that although things exist, they do not exist independently or inherently, you will be able to destroy the conception that things exist inherently.

So, these lines explain that although cause and effect function, they do not function in an inherent way. In fact inherent existence is the object of negation and it is what should be destroyed by true perception. This eliminates the extreme of permanence. In general, the whole of Buddhist teaching can be subsumed under four statements: all conditioned phenomena are impermanent, all contaminated things are suffering, all phenomena are empty and do not have self-existence, and nirvana is peace. From these four, it is clear that most schools of Buddhist tenets, with the exception of certain sub-schools such as the Vatsiputriyas, accept the explanation of selflessness.

The selflessness that is accepted by all the four different schools of tenets, is the lack of a self-supporting or self-sufficient person. The meaning of lack of substantial, self-supporting person is that there is no person who is completely independent of the mental and physical aggregates. If you view the mental and physical aggregates as the subject to be controlled and the person as the controller, and if you view this controller, a person, as something completely independent of those aggregates, you are maintaining a view of the existence of a substantial self-supporting person.

All four schools of Buddhist tenets accept that there is no such person independent of his physical and mental aggregates. This understanding weakens our strong yearning for the person, the enjoyer of happiness and suffering, to be something solid, but it seems that it is not very effective in weakening the attachment, anger and so on, that is generated by observing other objects of enjoyment. In general, attachment, hatred and so on, which are generated in relation to ourselves are stronger, so we think of my object of enjoyment, my relative, and my rosary.

If the object of enjoyment does not belong to you, then you may not have a very strong sense of an independent self-supporting person, but if you posses something then that feeling is stronger. This is clear if you compare the two attitudes before and after buying something, let us say a watch. First you buy it, then you start thinking 'this is my watch' and 'these are my clothes' and so forth. So because of that feeling of 'mine', the feeling of possessing that thing, you generate a very strong sense of the person to whom it belongs. Such a person is called substantially self-sufficient person. If you talk about nonexistence of such a substantial self-sufficient person, to people who have a strong sense of the existence of such a person, it will help reduce their attachment to their possessions.

In addition to this explanation of the selflessness of persons, when we study the highest schools of tenets, that is the Mind Only and Middle Way schools, we find subtler explanations of the selfessness not only of persons but also of phenomena. With respect to the Mind Only school's explanation, when we relate to different objects of enjoyment, such as form, and sound, they appear to us due to the awakening of imprints on our consciousness. So, according to the Mind Only explanation, all the various phenomena appear to us and we experience and enjoy them merely due to the awakening of the imprints left on the mind. In other words, all phenomena are of the nature of the mind and do not have any external existence.

This is one explanation of the meaning of emptiness and is a means to reduce attachment towards objects of enjoyment. But the Middle Way explanation is that no phenomena, whether the person, the enjoyer, or the object of enjoyment, exist inherently from their own side, because they are merely designated by thought. Thought designates name and then the phenomenon comes into being. Phenomena do not have an existence from their own side, other than being designated by the terms and thoughts of the mind. According to this explanation all phenomena have their own character and their own nature, but all these characteristics of specific phenomena exist in dependence on something else, they do not have a specific mode of existence from their own side.

Within the Middle Way School there are two interpretations of the meaning of emptiness. According to the Middle Way Autonomy School all phenomena exist, but their existence comes about as a product of two conditions. On the one hand a valid mind should designate the name and the term to that particular phenomenon, and at the same time the phenomenon should also exist from its own side. When these two conditions are met the phenomenon comes into existence. Other than being designated by the mind, there is no phenomena which come forth from their own side.

The subtlest explanation is found in the Middle Way Consequentialist school, which says that although there are things like form, sound, mountain, house and so forth that we can point to, they do not exist in the way we ordinarily perceive them. Usually phenomena appear to our consciousness as if they existed from their own side, but the Consequentialists say phenomena do not exist from their own side at all. They have only a conventional and a nominal existence. Therefore if phenomena existed in the way they appear to us, when we try to analyse, examine and find the object of designation, it should become clearer and clearer. But this is not so. When we try to analyse and examine the nature of phenomena we have perceived, we are unable to find them, instead they disappear. This shows that phenomena do not have any inherent existence and do not exist from their own side.

According to the Autonomy School the measure by which to prove that things exist, is existence from their own side. But the Consequentialists say things do not exist from their own side at all, because they are merely designated by the mind. For them a phenomenon's existence from its own side is the object of negation and the lack of such inherent existence or existence from its own side is the meaning of emptiness.

If you are able to perceive the real nature of phenomena by realising that they do not exist inherently, but in dependence on causes and conditions, such as designation by name and thought, you will have entered the path pleasing the Buddha. Usually when an object, form or sound, appears to us, it appears as if it has an independent or solid existence not dependent on causes, conditions, names, thoughts and so forth. But that is not real mode of existence. Therefore if you understand that they exist in dependence on these things and you thereby eliminate the misunderstanding that phenomena exist independently, you have understood the right path.

On the other hand, you might think about how all phenomena appear and the infallibility of their dependent arising, but be unable to generate the realisation that they are empty of inherent existence, or when you think about the emptiness of phenomena or their lack of inherent existence, you might be unable to accept the infallibility of their dependent arising. When you have to alternate these two understandings and are unable to think of them simultaneously, you have not yet realised the thought of the Buddha. As the following verse says,

> Appearances are infallible dependent arisings;
> Emptiness is free of assertions.
> As long as these two understating are seen as separate,
> One has not yet realised the intent of the Buddha.

Although phenomena do not have inherent existence, they have nominal existence. When we see the reflection of our own face in the mirror, the reflection is not the face itself. In other words, the reflection is empty of the real face because it is not the real face at all. Even though the reflection of the face is not the face because of the assembly of causes and conditions, the reflection of the face arises. The reflection is completely empty of being the real face and yet it is very much there. It was produced by causes and conditions and it will disintegrate due to causes and conditions. Similarly, phenomena have a nominal existence, although they have no existence independent of causes and conditions.

If you examine yourself or any other phenomena carefully in this way, you will find that although all phenomena appear to exist inherently, no phenomena exist from their own side or as they appear to us. However they do not have nominal existence which produces results, is functional and its activities are infallible.

> At the time when these two realisations are simultaneous and don't
>   have to alternate,
> From the mere sight of infallible dependent arising comes
>   ascertainment

Which completely destroys all modes of grasping.
At that time, the analysis of the profound view is complete.

If you familiarise your mind with this, a time will come when you do not have to alternate the two understandings: the understanding of the meaning of dependent arising and that of emptiness of inherent existence. Then you will understand the meaning of emptiness of inherent existence, by merely understanding the meaning of dependent arising without relying on any other reason. Merely by seeing that dependent arising is infallible, you will be able to destroy completely the misconception of the true existence of phenomena without relying on other conditions. When you are able to generate an understanding of dependent arising or emptiness of inherent existence as meaning the same, you have gained a complete understanding of the view of the real nature of phenomena.

Now we will complete the rest of the text of *The Three Principal Aspects of the Path*. When we think about the phenomena's lack of inherent existence, we should start our investigation with our own person and try to find out whether this 'I' or person has inherent existence or not. Find out who the person is and separate out the whole physical and consciousness aggregate by asking whether my brain is me, or my hand is me, or whether the other parts of the body are me. When analysed in this way, then the 'I' is unfindable. You cannot identify the 'I' with any of these factors, neither the whole physical body, or parts of it nor consciousness and its various levels.

If you think about the physical body itself and try to find out what it is, whether it is the hand and so forth, it will be unfindable. Similarly, if you analyse a particular table to find out what it is, whether it is its colour or its shape or the wood of which it is made, you will not be able to point to any particular quality of the table as the table.

When you are not able to find things through this mode of analysis, it does not mean that they do not exist. That would contradict reason and your own experience. Phenomena's unfindability under scrutiny indicates that they do not have any objective existence from their own side and that they do exist as posited or designated by the mind. There is no other way of establishing them. Since they do not have any objective existence independent of thought, their existence is dependent on the power of the object, the designation. Therefore, phenomena have a conventional or nominal existence.

But when you are not analysing or experimenting or studying in that particular manner and phenomena appear to you in their usual way, they appear to exist independently from their own side. It does not appear to you that they have only a nominal or conventional existence. But since you have some understanding through analysis and study, when things ordinarily appear to you as existing independently, you will be able to think, "Although phenomena do not have inherent existence, to my impure mind they appear to exist independently and inherently." In other words, if as a result of your study you compare phenomena's ordinary mode of appearance and the way things appear under investigation, you will understand the wrong way in which phenomena appear when you are not analysing them and then you will be able to identify the object of negation, inherent existence.

Therefore, when you are in an actual meditation session, it is important to ascertain through reasoning that things exist merely by designation and do not have an independent existence from their own side. However, as soon as you arise from meditation things will appear in the ordinary way. Then, due to the understanding you generated during the meditation session, even though phenomena appear as if they exist inherently or independently you will be able to confirm that although they appear in this way, this is not how they exist.

It is from this point of view that the next verse says:

Also, the extreme of existence is eliminated by the appearances
And the extreme of nonexistence is eliminated by the emptiness
And if the mode of the arising of cause and effect from emptiness is
    known,
You will not be captivated by the view that grasps at extremes.

This means that if you are able to understand that all phenomena exist conventionally, you will be able to eliminate the extreme of permanence, and by understanding that things do not have inherent existence, you will be able to eliminate the extreme of total nihilism or annihilation. In other words, you will be able to understand the nature of phenomena, that they exist conventionally and nominally but are empty of inherent existence. Due to their not existing inherently, things appear as causes and effects. If you are able to generate an understanding of such mode of existence, you will not be overpowered or captivated by the wrong view of the two extremes, that is permanence and nihilism.

Finally, the concluding verse says:

> Thus when you have realised the essentials
> Of the three principal aspects of the path accordingly,
> Seek solitude and generate the power of effort,
> And quickly actualise your ultimate purpose, my son.

The concluding advice is that it is not enough to have mere scriptural understanding. Having understood the meaning of the three principal aspects of the path, it is your responsibility to retire to an isolated place and put them sincerely into practice. Having understood the meaning of practice, you must engage in it with clarity because the aim and purpose of study is the attainment of omniscience, but it can only be gained through practice. So Jey Tsongkhapa advises us to practice well.

Therefore, as explained above, first establish some understanding of the view that phenomena lack inherent existence, then repeatedly make your mind familiar with that understanding so that through familiarity your ascertainment will become clearer, deeper, and stabler. Moreover, as our mind at present is strongly influenced by distraction and excitement, it is very difficult for it to stay calmly on one object even for a short time. Under such conditions even if you have realised the ultimate view it is difficult to make it manifest.

In order to have a direct perception of emptiness it is important to develop a calmly abiding mind through meditation. There are two techniques for doing so: one accords with the explanation you find in the sutras, and the other, which is found in the tantras, depends on deity yoga. this latter method is the more profound. In the tantras too, there are two levels, according to the deity yoga found in the lower classes of tantra and in the highest class of tantra.

In the Highest Yoga Tantra there is a special mode of doing deity yoga and achieving a calmly abiding mind by employing the subtle wind and the subtle mind. When you actualise calmly abiding mind through that process, what is known as a union of calm abiding and special insight into emptiness is achieved.

If we explain this union of special insight and calm abiding merely according to the nature of the meditative stabilisation, there is no certainty that it will become a cause of enlightenment. No doubt because of the attainment of special insight it is a Buddhist practice but it is less certain that the mere union of calm abiding and speical insight will become a cause of enlightenment. Whether it becomes a cause of liberation or omniscience depends on the motivation. Therefore we need a determination to be free from cyclic existence, as a foundation, and then, based on care and concern for the benefit of all sentient beings, an altruistic aspiration for enlightenment. If you then practise the yoga of the union of special insight and calmly abiding mind, it will become an active force for attainning enlightenment.

In order for such practice to be fruitful, it is important that you first receive tantric teachings. In order to receive tantric teachings to ripen your mental continuum, you must first receive initiation to make your mind fertile. Therefore, it is important to practise a combination of method and wisdom. When we engage in the altruistic aspiration to attain enlightenment for the sake of all sentient beings, it will influence and support the view understanding the real nature of phenomena, and in turn our realisation of emptiness, the real nature of the phenomena, will also influence and support our aspiration for enlightenment. This mode of practice is known as the union of method and wisdom.

When you follow the tantric path, you first generate a mind wishing to atttain enlightenment for the sake of all sentient beings, and then influenced by this altruistic aspiration, generate the wisdom realising emptiness, the real nature of phenomena, and on the basis of this realisation generate the deity. In other words, it is the wisdom apprehending the emptiness itself that is generated into the form of a deity. If you again focus on the nature of the deity itself, you will find that even the diety does not exist from its own side. Then you visualise the deity as the Truth Body that you will ultimately attain when you attain enligtenment.

So, the technique for meditating on both method and wisdom is very important and includes meditation on the extensive circle of the deity as well as on its profound emptiness. The unity of both method and the wisdom is involved in this tantric practice, because on the one hand you think about the nature of the deity itself, which is visualising the real nature of phenomena, and then on the other hand you think of the deity itself as the Truth Body that you will attain when you become enlightened, which is to think about the object of your attainment. So this is also a meditation on the aspiration for enlightenment.

Through this process of deity yoga you are practising both the method and wisdom at the same time. This is what makes the path so quick and successful. When you follow the Highest Yoga Tantra especially, there are techniques to make manifest the subtlest wind and subtlest consciousness. Through special techniques you will be able to stop the coarser, defiled levels of wind and consciousness and make their subtlest levels manifest.

Whether you follow the sutra or tantra path, if you want to practice in this way, you should first lay a solid foundation in the practice of morality or discipline.

There are many levels of discipline to be observed starting from the discipline of individual emancipation, which is like the foundation of all the higher levels of discipline. It is sometimes referred to as the discipline of the Hearers, and it is on the basis of this that you generate the discipline of the Bodhisattva, on the basis of which in turn you generate the disciple of Mantra.

Questions and Answers

Would Your Holiness clarify whether the determination to achieve liberation is not linked at all with the conception of true existence or the conception of phenomena as inherently existent?

Usually, when we talk about generating a strong wish to be free from cyclic existence, a mind wishing to attain liberation, with reference to a person who has really understood through study that there is such a thing as liberation and that it is something that can actually be achieved, who has a deep understanding based on reason, then we can say that his wish to attain liberation is not defiled by a conception of true existence or a conception of phenomena as inherently existent. This is because a person can usually have a valid cognition of liberation only after realising emptiness. If you have understood the meaning of emptiness, then even though you may not have uprooted the conception of true existence completely, neither the liberation that has to be established nor the path that establishes it are polluted by the conception of true existence or the conception of phenomena as inherently existent.

However, in the case of ordinary beings like us, who do not have a correct or authentic understanding of liberation's mode of existence, but merely a wish to attain it, while no doubt the wish is genuine, due to not understanding the real nature of phenomena, we might see liberation itself as truly or inherently existent. In other words, not having a good understanding of phenomena's lack of inherent existence, the wish to attain liberation is polluted by the conception of true existence.

In a verse of sutra the Buddha says that if on seeing the illusory image of a beautiful woman you feel a desire for her, it is foolish to regret it later when you realise that she was only an illusion, because there was no woman there in the first place. Similarly, if you think of liberation as truly existent, although it is not, then it is true to say that your aspiration towards liberation is not authentic.

Can we use a term like the bliss of liberation?

Yes, of course, because when we attain liberation, it is only the complete cessation of delusions. Otherwise one is still a person with a physical body. There is a feeling of pleasure and happiness of having attained liberation, although there is no craving for that blissful feeling. For example, if we speak in tantric terms then a superior individual being who has eliminated the conception of true existence has the wisdom of great bliss within this mental stream and that bliss is a real bliss. I think it is also appropriate to speak of the bliss of an individual at the stage of no longer training. So, we can say that even the Buddha has a feeling of pleasure and therefore we can speak of the bliss of liberation.

But if you are asking this question from the point of view of whether liberation itself is bliss, then it is not, because it is an impersonal phenomenon. Actually, liberation or cessation is a quality, a complete cessation of delusion within the particular person who has attained and actualised liberation. With reference to that person and when he or she attains liberation, it is the person himself or herself who experiences bliss. So, if you ask whether the person experiences the bliss of liberation, the answer is yes, but if you ask whether liberation itself is bliss, then the answer is negative.

How is meditation related to getting rid of the suffering of sentient beings?

When a bodhisattva actually engages in the training prior to enlightenment, he not only meditates on qualities like compassion and altruism, he actually engages in putting the six perfections into practice. Of the six perfections, giving and ethical discipline are directly related to the benefit of sentient beings. Similarly, a bodhisattva also engages in the four means of gathering disciples, such as giving things that sentient beings need, speaking pleasantly and so forth. The generation of compassion and love in meditation actually generates the intention and the practices of giving, observing ethical discipline and so on are the actual expression of that intention in action.

Therefore, practical application and meditation go together side by side. You will also find mention of the state of equipoise and the subsequent achievement. During meditative equipoise you engage in meditation and during the post-meditative state you arise from meditation and engage in collecting merit. This means practically engaging in activities that directly benefit sentient beings.

How is one's aspiration towards liberation related to the experiences of suffering?

In order to generate a wish to attain liberation, you should first be able to see the faults of cyclic existence. But at the same time if you do not have an understanding of the possibility of attaining liberation, then merely seeing the faults and sufferings of cyclic existence is not enough. There are many cases where people are faced with suffering, but are unaware of the possibility of attaining liberation. Not finding a solution to their problems, in frustration they commit suicide or harm themselves in other ways.

When the Hearer and the Solitary Buddhas have destroyed delusions completely and become Foe Destroyers, do they possess a neutral consciousness or neutral mind?

Yes, they have neutral consciousness. After having attained the status of a Foe destroyer, the Hearers and Solitary Buddhas not only have a neutral consciousness, but also employ other qualities like harsh speech and referring to others as inferior persons and so on. Although these kind of actions are not provoked by delusions like anger and attachment, they arise as a result of being well-acquainted with negative qualities in the past, which now expresses itself physically, verbally and mentally in bad ways.

People who have not realised emptiness see all phenomena as existing inherently and because of that they generate anger, attachment and so forth. But how do those people who have realised emptiness generate anger and attachment since the realisation of emptiness is a direct antidote to the experience of the conception of true existence?

The demarcation between these two experiences is that those who have realised emptiness do not have a conception of true existence which views things as inherently existent. Although things appear to them as inherently existent, they do not have a conception of true existence. Even to those who have attained higher grounds and become Foe Destroyers things appear to exist inherently. So there is no certainty that those for whom things appear to exist inherently should have attachment and anger. Therefore, anger and other delusions are generated not only when things appear to exist truly, but when there is also a determination that things have true existence. It is not possible to eliminate delusions and afflictions completely, merely by seeing emptiness or merely realising selflessness. You have not only to realise emptiness or selflessness, you also have to become well acquainted with it. When you not only understand but also see it directly, you attain what we call the path of seeing. An when you attain the path of seeing, you are able to temporarily suppress all superficial manifestation of delusions. Still you have only suppressed the manifestations of these delusions and have not finally eliminated their seeds. The innate delusions are still present.

Even after you have gained direct realisation of emptiness there are higher paths such as the path of seeing and path of meditation. Intellectually acquired delusions are those that are eliminated by the path of seeing and are thus eliminated when one sees emptiness directly. They come about as a result of studying mistaken philosophical ideas. In other words they are product of wrong views. When you see emptiness or ultimate reality directly, naturally intellectually acquired delusions, products of wrong view are automatically eliminated. Therefore, you have to become thoroughly familiar with this realisation of the true nature of phenomena. Then gradually as you attain the path of meditation, you will be able to eliminate the very root cause of delusions. Now, how is this conception of true existence, or the conception that things exist inherently, responsible for generating delusions like anger, attachment and so forth. Normally speaking it is not necessarily the case that wherever there is a conception of true existence delusions like attachment and anger are generated, because there are occasions when you have only a conception of true existence. But wherever there is attachment or anger it follows that it is due to a conception of the true existence of phenomena. When you generate attachment, you not only see the object as something interesting or attractive, but you see it as something totally attractive, totally interesting, and existing inherently from its own side. Because of that kind of misconception of phenomena, you generate a strong attachment.

Similarly, when you see something as uninteresting or unattractive, you do not see it just like that, you see it as totally uninteresting and unattractive. This is because you have a conception of the true existence of phenomena. The principal cause of all these different delusions, like attachment and anger, is the conception of 'I' and 'mine'. First you generate attachment towards the 'I' and because of this you start to generate all kinds of other delusions. Usually, you actually do not think about what this 'I' is, but when it arises automatically, you have a strong sense of an 'I' which is not just nominally existent, but a solid 'I' existing inherently from its own side.

Recognising the existence of a conventional 'I' is all right, but when you exaggerate it as having an independent existence it is wrong. That is the wrong view of transitory collection. Because you have that kind of conception of the 'I's' true existence, you generate other delusions like the conception of 'mine' thinking, "This or that is *mine*". When you have this conception of things as 'mine' you divide everything into two classes: those that you like, which you think of as mine, as interesting, as my friend and so on, based on which you generate a lot of attachment; and those that do not belong to you or that have harmed you or are likely to harm you, you classify into a different category and neglect them. Because of your conception of the 'I' and the feeling that you are somehow supreme, someone very important, you become proud. Due to this pride, when you don't know something you generate deluded doubt and when you encounter a challenge from people who have qualities or wealth similar to your own, you generate the delusions of jealousy and competitiveness towards them.

What is the meaning of a definite action and an indefinite action?

A definite action is one all of whose requisite parts are complete. For example, having made the preparations for doing a particular action, actually doing it and finally thinking that you have done the right thing. If you have committed an action through such a process, the result will be definite, so it is called a definite action.

On the other hand, if you have not generated the intention to commit a particular action, then even if you have done something, the result will not be definite. So, it is called an indefinite action. In general, there are many kinds of actions explained in the Asanga's *Compendium of Manifest Knowledge (Abhidharma Samuccaya)*: actions that are committed and not accumulated, actions that are accumulated and not committed and actions that are both committed and accumulated. Actions that are accumulated and not committed are definite actions. Actions that are committed and not accumulated are indefinite actions because, for example, of not being motivated.

Now, to explain this point more clearly, let us take the example of killing an animal. Generally speaking killing leads to bad rebirth. But if you kill a particular animal without intending to kill it, for instance if you unknowingly trample on an insect and kill it, but then realising what you have done you generate a strong sense of regret, the result will be indefinite. Because you have actually killed the insect you have committed the action of killing it, but you have not accumulated the action because you did not intend to kill it. In this case the result is not definite, which means that this act of killing will not lead to the normal result, bad rebirth, because of the absence of intention and having subsequently felt regret. However, since the act of killing was committed it will bear its own fruit. It does not lead to profit.

How is it possible, especially for a person who comes from the West to generate a sense of renunciation, an unwillingness to enjoy the pleasures of the world in which we are living?

It is not likely that everyone would generate a spirit of renunciation, nor is it necessary because of people's diverse mental interests and inclinations. Some take rather a fancy to cyclic existence. So what should we do? If we take the point of view of a Buddhist and strive to attain liberation, then we have to train the mind in this way. If you just glance at the Western way of life, you may see many superficial attractions, the ample modern facilities and so on. But if you examine it on a deeper level, Westerners are not immune to the general worldly sufferings of birth, old age, sickness and death, and are especially stricken with feelings of competitiveness and jealousy. I am sure that these disturb your happiness, so they are termed the sufferings of cyclic existence.

We can also classify suffering into three levels: the suffering of suffering; the suffering of change and pervasive compositional suffering. The last one, pervasive compositional suffering, refers to the fact that our physical body, projected by contaminated actions and delusions, itself acts as the basis for experiencing all the different levels of suffering. It is important to know the various levels and stages of sufferings and how to do meditation. In general, if you have no anxiety, no troubles and no worries, that is best. We think of practising the Buddha's doctrine because we have some suffering, some anxiety, but if you don't have these then there is no need to practice; just enjoy yourself.

Since we have this conception of a truly existent self, is it possible to benefit other beings?

It is possible. Actually there are two kinds of mistaken attitude with regard to the self: one is to hold it as inherently existent, the other is the self-centred attitude. If you have a very strongly self-centred attitude, perpetually concerned about your own well-being and nothing else, you will automatically neglect welfare of other beings. The conception of a truly existent self is difficult to get rid of, but while you are doing so you can also train in the altruistic attitude concerned with the welfare of other sentient beings and engage in activities to benefit them. Hearer and Solitary Foe Destroyers have destroyed the delusions with their seeds and have realised the real nature of phenomena. Thus they have eliminated the conception of true existence, but because of their self-centred attitude, they may not care much for the welfare of other sentient beings. However, it is also possible for a Bodhisattva, to belong to the Vaibhashika school of tenets, which does not assert emptiness of true existence. So, although that Buddhisattva may not have eliminated the seed of the conception of true existence, but because he has trained in developing an attitude of concern for others, he will work with total dedication for the benefit of other sentient beings.